a sound mind

the rebirth

stacie p. calvin

S.H.E. PUBLISHING, LLC

A Sound Mind : The Rebirth
Copyright © 2021 by Stacie P. Calvin.

All rights reserved. Printed in the United States of America. No part of this book may be used or reproduced in any manner whatsoever without written permission except in the case of brief quotations embodied in critical articles or reviews.

For information contact :

W : **www.shepublishingllc.com**

E : **info@shepublishingllc.com**

Book Cover and Title Page Design by Michelle Phillips of CHELLD3 3D VISUALIZATION AND DESIGN

ISBN :

978-1-953163-13-4 (paperback)

978-1-953163-14-1 (*She*Edition)

First Edition : May 2021

10 9 8 7 6 5 4 3 2 1

My Dedication is to my GRANDchildren:

My Legacy:
TLK

My**T**ruBeauty

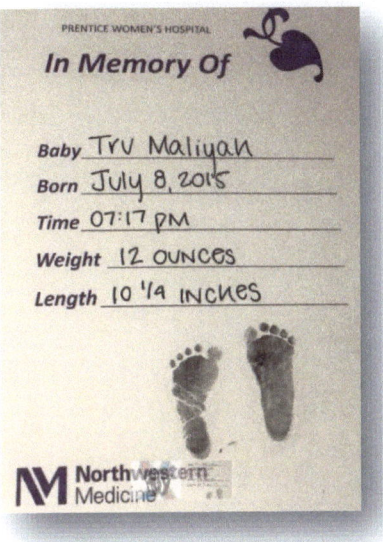

MyFly:
Legend Kannon

MyPinky:
Kacie Jae

CONTENTS

SYNOPSIS VII
THE ADVENTURE 1
THE JOURNEY 20
THE NEED 44
THE GIFT 56
THE JOY 69
SYNOPSIS 97
AKNOWLEDGEMENTS 99
MEET THE AUTHOR 103

Synopsis

"Right now, in your possession, you have a little extra, a resource, a talent, a gift ready to be given. You are blessed. You are a blessing. However, there's a problem, an issue, a hurt, a wound somewhere in the world that only you can heal, no matter how inadequate you feel. Your inner satisfaction, ultimate fulfillment, purpose and true happiness will never be fully unlocked until your unique gift, and the world's unique need come together. That's the key that will unlock God's story in your life; it will transform ordinary life into an extraordinary adventure. The difference between ordinary and extraordinary is just that little *extra*."

To see God's vision in your life, there are four promises you must claim.

- You have a **gift** only you can give;
- Someone has a **need** only you can meet;
- The **journey** is where the gift and the need collide; and
- The fourth promise will be revealed later in this book.

These promises are true for everyone everywhere, and we'll unpack them in detail in this book. Are you ready for an adventure?

a sound mind

the rebirth

stacie p. calvin

The Adventure

The Beginning of My Story

Text Message to My Son & Daughter (Me):
My surgery is scheduled for tomorrow at 7 a.m., a couple of hours. If I may fall into a deep sleep, it is God's plan. Don't make a big fuss. You both know that I want to be cremated. No service is needed. I have insurance, and would rather my Grandchildren split that money. No waiting for people to come in from out of town. I'm not "traditional"; I'm working on a Living Will. You both need to know that NO debts will Be left for your responsibility. I LOVE YOU BIG, MY TWO MOST LIFE-CHANGING GIFTS.

Son (TJ):
"Everything will go well."

Daughter (MyME):
"God is watching over you mommy. Talk to you before and after. I love you."

STACIE CALVIN

> **Daughter (MyME):**
> "Father God, I come to you now with an open heart; I ask that you cover every doctor, surgeon and medical staff that will be preforming on my mother today. I know that you already have it covered. I bind every negative feeling and thought in the name of Jesus! In Jesus' Name, Amen."

I was transported to the hospital by Emergency Medical Technicians (EMTs), where labs, EKG, and chest X-rays were performed. My veins collapsed, my blood clotted, and my right arm was bruised. A blood thinner was administered along with an insulin shot through my stomach, and my pressure was being monitored through my legs. At that moment, I thought I was experiencing a heart attack.

While in the hospital bed, I began reflecting on everything that happened two weeks prior. I'd undergone surgery, my son had been arrested, and my daughter-in-love (mother of my granddaughter) had gone to urgent care with complaints of sharp pains in her chest. EMTs transported her to the hospital for overnight observation; they thought it would be best to monitor her heart. She has a heart condition. I was comparing her experience to what I was currently experiencing, being hooked up to IVs and monitors, and that's why I thought I was having a heart attack.

How This All Began

I'd undergone surgery on my left elbow due to damaged nerves. Two weeks after surgery and being sunken into the couch with depression, wondering why I wasn't being cared for like I expected to be, I phoned my SheroSisterHope to come by to bathe me. She would always bathe me after one of my many unfortunate turn-of-life events. We'd laughed about my comment because she lives in Chicago, and I now live in Texas. So instead, MyLifePartner drew me a hot bath, and he would bathe me this time around.

The anxiety, sadness, stress, worry, and fear were coming off in layers. If you know me, you know I am anti-medication. I told MyME how I didn't particularly like how the acetaminophen-HYDRO condone, prescribed for pain after the surgery, made me feel. It was making me feel like the

Vicodin made her feel when it was prescribed to her for pain when she tore her ACL freshman year of high school. As an inside joke between her and I, we call Vicodin "the Viagra." She later overcame opioids by being a three-sport student-athlete going on to compete at the collegiate level as a Heptathlete.

I discontinued taking the prescribed medication on the third day and began taking 800mg ibuprofen for the pain. While getting the ibuprofen from the basket of medicines, I left the bottle of tramadol, acetaminophen-HYDRO condone, and Sulfamethoxazole trimethoprim out on the tray next to the couch where I had been lying.

I remember repeating to my son to promise me that he wouldn't have me committed because I knew I was off balance, and I felt delirious from taking all of the different medications I was prescribed. I would later Face-Time MyME, having her promise me that she wouldn't allow her brother to have me committed.

My daughter-in-love had never been to Red Lobster, thinking they only served seafood, which she doesn't eat. My girlfriend and I went there after my pre-op. I remember us discussing going there on Valentine's Day because my son was going to propose with my mother's ring. My mother made this promise to her first grandson.

Two days before surgery, one of my favorite DJs was coming to Dallas from Chicago. I knew I would be down for a while in the near future, so I needed some Dance Therapy! I remember saying, "let me dance it off," except there was no music playing. House Music all night long would be ringing in my ears.

I then said to my son, "Tell your Godmother, which is MyGoodJudy, that 'Moo' is coming out of her coma." Moo is a sister-friend of mine whose been in a coma for a couple of months. I remember speaking that aloud, but it was me coming out of the coma that I thought I was in. Frightening MyME, she called her Godmother, which is MyBestie. I don't remember talking with her, nor do I remember talking to MyCaliBeauty niece in California, but I remember hearing, "What did she take?" I guess I was trying to explain what I had taken. I'm not sure what I was saying because all I heard was laughter. I had no visual sight as to who was laughing. TV shows and commercials were replaying in my head.

I remember hearing voices repeatedly, things like the staff introducing themselves. MySheroSister Hope was on speakerphone. The last voice I remember hearing was hers, stating, "She could be like that for life." I remember yelling out, but no one could hear me, thinking, *I'm tripping; this is all in my head.* No one heard a damn thing that I was saying. Why? I went into a non-responsive blank stare.

Out of the overflow of the heart, the mouth speaks is what I thought to myself. I remember that scripture from Matthew 12:34 in the King James Version of the bible. I thought I was under anesthesia and that I fell into a deep sleep, reliving my life from 2014 to the present 76 times in reverse.

Concerned for my mental state, my sisters made the executive decision to have my son call the EMTs.

At the Hospital

I thought I was in a mental institution. I remembered repeatedly being asked my name, my date of birth, and where I was. The bright light was shining in my face. The EMTs asked all the questions you would ask a person showing signs of Psychosis, which is a mental disorder characterized by a disconnection from reality. I remember changing rooms within the hospital. I thought I was waking up from the anesthesia.

Delusional about my whereabouts, I knew my name and my date of birth. I knew it was February; I didn't know the day or the year. My son had my mother, the Duchess, on the phone, and she'd begun giving the doctor my medical history. My mother also mentioned to the doctor that she was allergic to Sulphur and that I may be allergic to that. MyDuchess would usually experience the same side effects: anxiety, blurred vision, bruising, swelling, and dizziness.

Another antibiotic was administered intravenously. It was going to take 24-hours for the medication to eliminate from within my system. All the medicines caused a chemical imbalance. I was hallucinating from the narco. I was having a conversation with a male nurse and the male x-ray technician, thinking I was conversating with the male techs from my surgery that happened two weeks prior. I also called the nurses on staff by the "crew names" from the surgery.

After three days of being awake (literally), living my life out loud 76 times in reverse, I finally went to sleep! MyLifePartner and my son were taking shifts being at my bedside. When I woke up in the hospital, I expected the clock to read 2:30 PM and be at my home in my bed talking to my Duchess on the phone. I was hallucinating and remembering when my great-niece was institutionalized due to a chemical imbalance from the medications she takes daily for her Epilepsy.

The reality was beginning to settle in. I wasn't in an intuition. I was in a hospital! I no longer recognized the doctor as my surgeon, greeting him with a smile of shame.

"You're smiling, you feeling better, can you tell me your name?" the doctor asked.

"Stacie Calvin!" I replied.

"Where are you?" said the doctor.

Chuckles SMH., "I'm in the hospital," I replied in disbelief that this wasn't all a dream.

The doctor asked, "Why are you here?"

"My family wasn't sure what I had taken. I didn't overdose! I love myself too much to do that," I replied. I looked down at my phone case with **MyFly** and **MyPinky**, their first-time meeting photo on it. I kept it with me throughout my adventure. My GRANDchildren brought me back. They are My Legacy.

The doctor continued to ask me questions.

"Are you dizzy?" he drilled.

"I have a headache," I replied.

"Have you eaten?" he continued.

"No," I said.

"Let's see if we can get you some breakfast, something for your headache, and get you discharged," he reassured.

Shortly afterward, I made my way to the bathroom. This was my first time going to the toliet without assistance, thinking, *'Why am I wearing the hospital "designer panties"? I'm menopausal! Giggles. Ah!' That's why the nurses were cleaning me up—* remembering the conversation that my SheroSister Hope and I had about bathing me. All the trauma caused a cycle to flow. I took the medication for my headache then fell asleep, only to be awakened by my body rejecting the meds. I never did get that breakfast, and I should not have taken that medication on an empty stomach.

As the nurse cleaned the hospital room, the phone rings. She answers the phone and hands it to me; it's my son.

"We're on our way up there, getting the baby ready," he announces.

I fell asleep again. Awakening to my Life Partner's face, I began to question if this was reality. I thought he came to get me instead of my son. He thought my son was with me already and was coming to relieve him. Lines of communications were crossed. They forgot whose shift it was to sit with me. Everyone was sleep-deprived. I kept the household awake with my 3-day episode of Dreams vs. Reality.

A SOUND MIND

> *Many studies have been and are being done by Psychologists to find the connection between dreams and reality. Dreams are a product of the subconscious being awake during your thinking. The dream can affect your thoughts. Soothing dreams make you feel good in sleep, as well as in reality.*
>
> *-Oura*

"Heyyyy! I can go home," I said

"Did the doctors say you can go home today?" replied MyLife Partner.

"Yes! I'm going home today," I replied. I sounded like Diana Ross in the movie *Lady Sings the Blues* when Louis McKay came to get Billie Holiday after they killed Piano Man. I felt like she was, too, still a little loopy.

The doctor went to sign the discharge papers. As I was getting dressed, associating going home in the hospital gown from the surgery, it occurred to me that I only had on my housecoat, the "designer panties," and the socks from the hospital to go home in.

I'm Discharged! The nurses escorted me down, this time on the elevator, in a wheelchair to the front door. There waiting was my Life Partner to take me home. During the drive, I called my Son to let him know that I was on the way home.

Finally at Home

After settling in, things were still a blur after arriving home. All I wanted were shrimp tacos that my son fed to me. Apparently, that's the last thing that I had eaten before my episode began. I remembered that they were good.

While my daughter-in-love sautéed the shrimp, preparing to make the tacos, I began asking questions. While eating, my family wouldn't allow me to revisit anything that happened. The subject was off-limits.

They heard it 76 times; enough was enough. My son even threatened me that if I didn't go and lay down, that he was "going to call them people to come to get me." Grateful I have grandchildren now, I would jokingly state that I know my son is going to put me in a nursing home, that he should make sure it's a good one. He took great care of me during this adventure.

> *Embrace uncertainty. Some of the most beautiful chapters in our lives won't have a title until much later.*
>
> -Bob Goff

The day before my favorite niece's 30th birthday (MyFavNiece is what I call her), I made a post on Facebook but deleted it after I texted her. She replied

"Thank you, Fave. You do know that's it's tomorrow?"

We laughed about it as if I knew I wasn't going to be around for her birthday.

Out of curiosity, I went into the fitness room. BEHOLD... the dream was revealed. It was my 2014 Vision Board (wall); that year, I had my vision on a wall.

Trapped in my thoughts, there are 15-30 images, 3-5 chapters, 76 pages, trying to figure out the significance of the numbers, overthinking how I can bring this dream into reality. My family wouldn't fill me in on the blanks, and I couldn't remember anything. Fueled with fear, I Facetimed MyDuchess, sharing what the dream had revealed, stating that some things were detailed.

"The memory of the righteous is blessed. You will remember what you need to remember," she said.

Duchess prayed KJV 2 Timothy 1:7 *For God hath not given us the spirit of fear; but of power, and of love and of a sound mind.*

At the time, I didn't have a title for this book. Wow Duchess! That's it! You just gave me the title, *A Sound Mind*.

We were on a spiritual high. When I shared with my household that my son is supposed to go to school to become a male nurse, he had been a Mental Health Tech for the job that closed its doors. My daughter-in-love was going to stay home with MyPinky until she turned six months. Instead, she starting a new career. They were not as enthusiastic about my reality, thinking I was still imbalanced, requesting that I rest, relax and get some sleep. I began thinking that I was still imbalanced myself; things were still a blur. I took their advice, stating to myself *you are not your diagnosis* (Allergies and adverse reactions altered my mental status).

Before I laid down, fearful that I wouldn't get my memory back, I prayed:

A SOUND MIND

Fill my heart and mind with your peace. Give me wisdom and insight into the next steps towards complete freedom and victory within my mental and emotional health.

While I sat at home filling out paperwork for workman's compensation and sipping my tea for pain and anxiety, I anxiously awaited the news regarding my son and if he would be detained. He was in possession of an unknown substance. Some time had passed, and my daughter-in-love texted me that court was continued. She said, "we're on the way to the house to tell you about your granddaughter talking while court was in session. When they arrived, they expounded upon the story. We laughed and the last thing I remembered before passing out was talking to My Duchess around 2:30 PM on the phone.

The Next Morning

"I woke up this morning,

Realizing I

Don't have

What it takes

To sit back and

Be average. I

Was born for GREATNESS..."

Unknown

I reached out to my success partner (My ViSister) and shared with her what was on my heart.

She said, "I never published a book before. Send it over, and let me pray on it to see if God is placing this on my heart to do."

This will be a first for both of us. I then sent the Synopsis

"Well now. Let's do it!"

Okay, I have to type it all out. I have it written in my journal. I didn't want to depart from it. I was giving myself until the end of March. I became anxious to see so many others books unfolding; it was taking a little longer than I anticipated.

I sent an unfinished manuscript to the individuals that God placed on my heart to send it to. In the dream, the release of the book wasn't until a year later. The thing is, I'm not confident what year I was in. God's timing is always perfect.

After receiving a family group text that My Duchess was admitted into the hospital, I blamed myself, putting the book on hold. It's easy to get discouraged and give up. God wants us to be so full of hope that we can't help believing in The Best. "God, I AM asking for Your Best in my life."

The Duchess was discharged from the hospital after three days. She was assuring me that I didn't cause her to visit the hospital.

The book was on pause. Doubt kills more dreams than failure ever will. I decided that this adventure was going to be another one of my Facebook posts. Every time I got ready to post, 'what's on your mind?' I was prevented from doing so. On the first attempt, my phone went black for a couple of days. One the second attempt, after getting the phone repaired, it jumped off the table.

Yes! It jumped. That's when I looked around to see if anyone else noticed that, but I'm the only one in the room. *Okay, I hear you!* I didn't attempt to share "what was on my mind" anymore. I am allowing the guidance to let my pencils flow.

I began reading a 7-day devotional. 'Fighting for Mental and Emotional Health.' Each day was throwing out the negative thoughts. A quote from the devotion:

"The greatest battle you will ever fight in your life is between your ears."

Day 7 Choose Life

I began declaring that God has a purpose and destiny for my life. That HE loves me, and HIS plans are for good, not evil. I was giving my thoughts power to produce peace, joy, gratitude, love, and freedom.

Taking a Blessing Inventory, I started in one closet, where I thought I had eaten the edible, constantly going back to the scene of the crime. I was sorting through some of my overflow of clothes and shoes that I was no longer wearing, and I came across an old journal. The opening page reads:

2014 Houston Vitality Sept. 12-13 I came with expectancy for this journal. They were sold out. My Success Partner presence got her and myself Life Health Prosperity Journal.

Seeing your goals written in your handwriting has a powerful effect on your mind. So much of my LIVE LIST by Fifty had already been written in the journal. I continued journaling as I came to a nugget from my Vi Sister, "Choosing to Succeed- Success Slayer don't let Procrastination •Disbelief •Unforgiveness Keep you from being successful." The first chapter, *The Adventure*, was completed.

THE JOURNEY

> Everybody has a Unique Path

My journey from about 2018 to 2020 was made up of several different events that I will share with you. These events include significant people in my life. This part of my story begins with me going through my journal, checking to see where my head had been. There were empty pages at first, with the words 'Jill Scott's Prepared' written on them. So I listened to the lyrics of the song. I also came across something I had written to myself in 2014 before I relocated to Texas:

You don't have to try and figure it all out! I feel your heart. I have a plan for you. Your name is Stacie, which means Resurrection; fruitful. You are not your past. You didn't cause pain in others' hearts. It is not your job to try and heal them. You pray for them and move on. Stay Focused! You have lives to change. You stated that you wanted to grow your business, get your own place and car (paid for by a previous company). You are building a legacy for your children and their children. Life insurance is needed!... Reestablish credit. Continue to live below your means. You are a Go-Getter! (Goal Getter) Now get up and take action! Use your resources.

I stuck it in the back of my journal. That is precisely what I had been doing, getting prepared. I now have all those things. 2014 I was in great health. I accepted the Challenge, transformed.

I relocated to Texas, where I began to live my life out loud on purpose with purpose from the inside out (#DivinebyDesign). Those were my hashtags throughout my transformation.

My Mantra

RISK

BY FRANK WATSON

DO NOT BE AFRAID TO SHINE.

THIS WORLD NEEDS WHAT YOU HAVE TO GIVE.

OPEN UP THE AREAS OF YOUR BEING.

EXPOSE THEM TO YOURSELF–TO OTHERS.

You are valuable

You are unique

You have much to give.

Do not be afraid to give it.

As we risk ourselves, we grow.

Each new experience is a risk; we can try, and maybe fail, and as a result, grow or hold back and stagnate.

You have the potential to be anything you want to be!

You are free to choose

You are limited only by your fears.

Let your dreams take over. Fly with the eagles;

soar into life. The world is waiting for you!

Experts estimate that we have anywhere between 50,000 to 80,000 thoughts a day. My question for you is this. Have you ever thought about what you are thinking about? If left unchecked, our thoughts dictate our lives. Thoughts have the power to bring anxiety, stress, worry, sadness, and fear into our hearts. They also have the power to produce peace, joy, gratitude, love, and freedom in our lives. It's our choice.

STACIE CALVIN

Trauma That Caused Disconnect

I begged my son and the mother of my first granddaughter (My TruBeauty) after being born to talk to someone. Being their support system returning to Texas, sitting at the bottom of the pool, was how I dealt with the two trauma events months apart in my life. I had a disconnection after holding My TruBeauty's tiny lifeless body in my hand and dealing with the death of my dad, DaddyDell. DaddyDell is not my biological father. My father died. I knew of him; however, we didn't have the opportunity to get to know each other. DaddyDell took me as his own. Everyone knew this, including his daughters, who befriended me.

DaddyDell's daughters planned to lure me shopping; they were going to jump me, which was later revealed by one of the wicked stepsisters. I wasn't leaving MyDuchess' side. That was why I came to support MyDuchess. So then, it was decided that they would jump me at the memorial service. That plan was not carefully thought out. UNBOTHERED, all of my sisters, nieces, my daughter, and cousins had my back. We were that family about to fight at the funeral. After all of the commotion, we managed to get through the service. DaddyDell didn't want a service. The family joke is that he's looking at us, stating, "Stupid MotherFuckers". We laughed about it;

A SOUND MIND

Daddy Dell's favorite saying…………….. "Stupid motherfuckers", can't nobody say it as he can.

> Sometimes it takes an overwhelming breakdown to have an undeniable breakthrough.

Toast to a New Year

Happy New Year 2019, the Year of Making It Happen! The year started rocky—me having surgery and having two streams of income. However, no income was streaming in. My son was losing his income. The household was depressed. Life seemed a little dull and cloudy. I was researching for my book, soughting out the Dreams vs. Reality episodes I was experiencing, redirecting my energy towards my story. Depression can feel all-consuming.

From February 2019 to October 2019, it was all a blur. I was going through the motions. Everyone in the household was back working except for me. However, I did have an income coming in from workman's compensation. I was going to therapy and bonding with my granddaughter (MyPinky). There was a lot of tension in the house.

It wasn't easy holding it all together while focusing on getting MyPinky and her mother to Chicago safely. My son had already gone before them. My belongings were in a storage unit, my tire was on a flat, and my car needed mechanical repairs. I decided to deal with it when I returned.

It was MyPinky's 1st birthday. The plan was always to celebrate her birthday in Chicago. Her parent's plan to move back to Chicago was for her maternal grandmother to keep her. However, MyPinky's maternal grandmother was ill and later died in March of 2020, right at the beginning of the pandemic. I just wanted to bring MyPinky back to Texas with me.

Waiting for approval for an apartment, I got a room through the *Hotel Tonight* app for a couple of days.

A SOUND MIND

> *"Your life reflects much of what you think about and feel. If you find that you are in situations that are too uncomfortable or unpleasant, it may be a sign that you are out of alignment with who you truly are. Take some special time to uncover your deepest desires and the root of your thoughts. Take Action! Soon, your life will begin to transform to reflect who you truly are at Your Best! With time, you'll come to see that the frantic, broken, anxious, unhinged version of you was nothing to be ashamed of. You were simply a kindhearted person reacting to a very unkind situation."*
>
> The Black Butterfly

When challenges arise in your life, it is essential to have a strong support system. Sorting out mentally what is needed to move past life's challenges is often difficult to articulate. "Black PEOPLE... it's ok to go to counseling or therapy! It is! And no, it does NOT make you crazy. It makes you wise" I would not have known that I had a disconnection.

STACIE CALVIN

> *The way we've been trying to heal and be healed is with these topical, surface, superficial, temporary solutions. I'm telling you; true healing is from the inside out. We've been told to protect our outer man while our inner man is dying*
>
> —Lauryn Hill

"MOVING ON"
sounds easy.

but i died a thousand times in pain just to appreciate this phrase.

Prayer of Focus

I pray you would bring the right people across my path and deepen my relationships with family and friends. Use the people around me to encourage my heart.

A SOUND MIND

Everyone you meet plays a part in your story. Some may take a chapter, others a paragraph, but most will be no more than scribbled notes in margins. Someday, you'll meet someone who will become so intergalactic to your life, you'll put their name in the title.

Unknown

"Ever have a moment when you sit and take in an amazing moment and say, "Wow, how did I get here?"

God has a purpose for you and will move you even while being still. You will end up in positions that you never applied for. Stay prayerful, stay positive and no matter what, stay Humble.

#PositiveVibes #Encourage

Sometimes God closes

doors because it's time to

MOVE forward. He knows you won't move unless your circumstances force you. Trust the transition. Gods got you!!"

Authoress Sylvia

I reached out Authoress Sylvia and shared how I was missing the journey to my story. I explained how I reached out to my Ex for his consent to share our story. The funny thing is that he, too, was writing a book. Authoress suggested that we Co-Author together. Trying to manage everyone else's emotions, I suppressed my own, and the book was on pause.

> "I had to make you uncomfortable, otherwise you never would've moved."
> - God

I reached out to another one of my success partners, whom I also refer to as My ViSister. We shared a conversation we had in April 2016.

A SOUND MIND

"Hello, my sister in Christ, my Sista for life," I said. I continued by saying, "I journaled the past 12 years of my marriage. However, after we divorced, I burned them."

"This may sound crazy, but to answer your question, start writing," said My ViSister. "God will establish every word that needs to be spoken from your heart! This is your season to get that book from your heart and into the hands of women who are crying out for help. Allow God to be the Co-Author of your story, and it will come forth. Time to PUSH that baby out, Greatness!"

In all caps, I read:

DEAR HEALED WOMAN,

IT'S TIME TO HELP OTHER WOMEN FIND THEIR HEALING.

GOD HAS BROUGHT YOU TOO FAR

TO NOT HELP EMPOWER

ANOTHER WOMAN

-Unknown

Whoa...

STACIE CALVIN

September 2020 is when I read the Facebook post below.

> It's finally here! "September" month 9 which means it's birthing time! Just as a women who have been pregnant and waiting for her full term delivery. It's birthing time 🐣 🐣 🐣 I feel like I have a word for you. Called "Push" push past your disappointments, failures, and hurts. Make up in your mind month 9 is my time. I'm speaking to all my dreamers and action takers! As a wife coach my job is to help those who have been called to the office of being a wife! Single, married, or currently divorce. It doesn't matter your current title. The reason you want to push is because you want to grow, and do things different. "Hey I get it" I can hear you whispering to yourself " Help me be a better wife"
>
> I help women discover being happy and healthy wives. So that, they are better versions of themselves.
>
> Maybe your still waiting on Mr. Right or perhaps your laying next to him every night and yet you also need to push to keep those flames burning. Sis, "PUSH" Until we chat tomorrow about "creating a happy marriage begins with intention" have a restful evening and talk with you tomorrow 😉
> #newbeginings #newmonthnewgoals #wivesandmothers #marriedwithchildren #singlemomsclub #marriedcouples #womeninbusiness #mompreneurlife

I knew it was time for delivery. See, when I met Ivana, I was newly divorced, focused; my heart was healed. My daughter was entering her first year of college, and I was turning 40. Fast-forward ten years (embarking on 50), I needed to get back to that space, re-learn what I learned, that the spiritual journey had nothing to do with being nice. It was about being genuine, authentic, having boundaries, honoring my room first, others second. In this self-care space, being nice just happened. It flowed, not motivated by fear but by love. Let your voice be heard.

Mr. Stacy & Mrs. Stacie

My past is my past. I will not be held hostage to it. Twice too many times, it was tried against me, but the Teeheehee was on them. Both my Ex and I were healed from allowing the enemy to use a skit that we were gifted in a mime form, acted out in real life to destroy our marriage. We became "Swingers." The swinging swung too far without my knowledge. On the morning after his confession, I was pissed and, on my way, out of the door for work.

"We'll talk about this when I get home!" I spoke. I got a call at my place of work telling me that my husband is cheating on me. Was I interested in what she had to say? No! Our rule number 1 was *there's nothing anyone can tell us about one or the other*. "You bought that lie." When I got home, I said, "You gave her power over me; she knew too much about me!'

The following day, she called back. Here's where she put the "fu fop" on me. I wasn't talking to who I thought I didn't want to talk to in the first place. I was talking to mistress number 2. Needless to say, the 12-year marriage dissolved in a divorce.

Some might say I share too much; the thing of it is, as I like to state, I can tell my story better than anyone else can. You might leave out the juicy parts, which you'll read all about. My ex-husband and I decided to take Authoress up on her suggestion to co-author together. The ugly part of your story will be the most powerful part of your testimony.

More Confirmation on Social Media

Dr. Makeba Facebook post:

"Fill in the blank: In order to live my best life in this season,

I MUST_____!!

My comment to her post:

Share My Gift

I began reading Dr. Makeba's book entitled *Unapologetically Me*. The spirit said...*Not until you write your own*. I looked over in the direction where my journals were. Then I began to receive more confirmations.

My friend Joyce's Facebook post:

Let me say this, and then you can carry on about your day! Faith without works is dead. If you are passionate about something, please don't wait around for someone to hook you up or give you a connection, you have to go out and network, introduce yourself to the people who have what you want! Make your request known to God! Please don't sit on a dream and expect it to magically come to life; don't fear what people have to say. Matter of fact, don't care what people have to say! Some people fear your power, so don't get upset when they don't support you or even talk about you. Let your success speak on your behalf! Just don't give up! Oh, and keep some things to yourself until it's time to reveal! Ok, carry on. I'm so happy right now!

Then *A Purpose Driven Woman* was released. Joyce co-authored on this book. I purchased it, and as I began to read it, I heard the spirits say again... *Not until you write your own.*

STACIE CALVIN

VA's Facebook post about daily Words to live by:

"Let go of your story so the

The universe can write a new one for you."

Marian Williamson

I began to do just that!"

        Set some goals

        Stay quiet about them

        Smash the shit out of them

        Clap for your damn self

My DJ (VA) had been very instrumental from the beginning of my healing journey when he came to Texas to DJ two days before my elbow surgery and now with his virtual House Music parties. Zigzag is where he changes the frequency, yet it is still good. He asks permission in the chat, and we say YES! Receiving a notification from Twitch was the highlight of my day. "It's a virtual party." House music is a spiritual thing, a body thing, and a soul thing. Music is healing.

A SOUND MIND

I Am Becoming Mindful of Who I Am

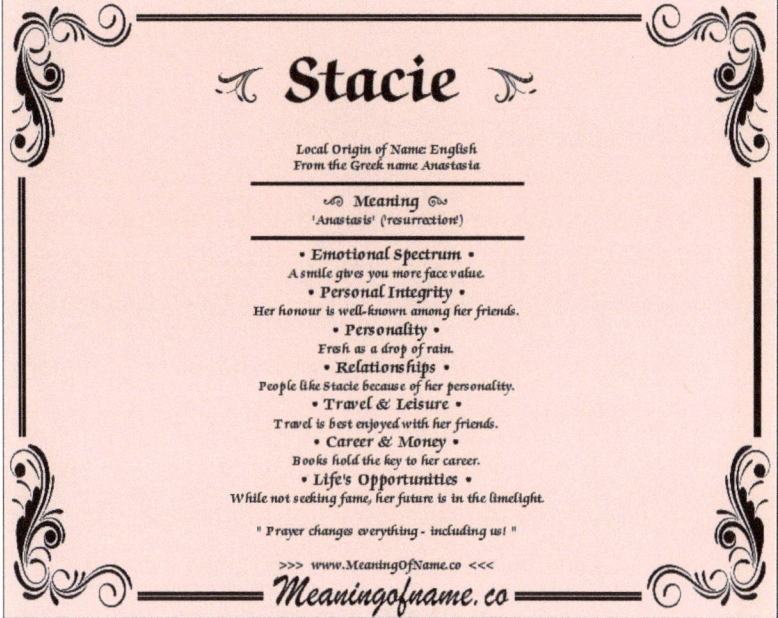

Another question that was asked from the WaKanna Business Massive Action Challenge is, "What are you willing to fight for?"

God is fighting for you. You have to do your part in the natural. Fight to wake up, don't dream your life. Live your dream. Rise Anastasia! My name in Greek, and when I have intimate and personal time with God, that's what HE calls me.

Today I choose to fight to be fully alive! Please give me the energy to live this day to the fullest. Please help me to be present and engaged with the people in my life. Thank You for Your Life and energy at work in my heart and mind.

> **Facing Reality**

The Adventure was not all glitz and glamor. I revisited some ugly truths from my dark past. See, I had said some things throughout the Dreams vs. Reality episode. Ill feelings were harbored towards me. It was coming up on the anniversary of Dreams vs. Reality. MyLifePartner had a trigger that led him to put me out of his house. See, not many people knew that MyLifePartner had put me out, nor was it known that my memory had lapsed. I was trying to figure it out until I wasn't. During the episode, I threw MyLifePartner "under the bus."

After MyLifePartner received a message telling him of some things that I stated about him, 'which they were stated' (third party information) kind of like Denzel in the movie *Ricochet*. I said that, but I didn't say that, not to that person, not at the time when it was stated that I was at a location. MyLifePartner felt that I would "Fork him over, make him look like a fool, paint him out to be the wrong person." As I did during my episode, I hurt him, not intentionally! I had no clue what I was saying or what I said.

He showed me a picture of a ring some weeks before this incident occurred, stating that it wasn't the ring that I had chosen and that he only had one more payment left to pay on it. This convinced me to believe that I didn't need to see if the third time marrying was a charm.

Outdoor Weddings

In Dreams vs. Reality, I remembered planning two weddings that were outdoor events. At this time, I was at sea celebrating my brother's 25th Wedding Anniversary while My BFF was in the States having a BA/Surprise Engagement Celebration.

I made a post, "I'm Getting Married in Jamaica 2019." After receiving over 200 congratulatory messages, I didn't dare to correct the lie (speaking things into existence). The pandemic saved face for me. The lie cost me My BFF.

STACIE CALVIN

> **Face reality as it is, not as it was or as you wish it to be.**
> Jack Welch

Bathrooms have mirrors for reasons other than taking a "selfie." We keep focusing on getting the right angles to capture that perfect image before changing what we don't like to see. We delete the images. Why is that? I'll share why; I believe that we don't want to expose the complex challenges in our lives.

The Naked Truth

I don't care who I lose anymore as long as I don't

lose myself again. To thy self be true; it gets messy in the middle. Sometimes you need something to ease the pain. My choice is music, Mirror Dance - Afefe Iku is my feel-good song. DON'T BE AFRAID TO GET NAKED! When you're naked, there's nothing to hide behind that makes you feel vulnerable. Every perceived imperfection screams out for the kind of attention you don't want. Get naked and let the world see the real YOU for you. However, "GETTING NAKED" may not have anything to do with clothing and your body, but rather EVERYTHING to do with you being genuine and upfront with YOURSELF. When you face things as YOURSELF, you can work with what's in front of you to either accept them or change them.

The Pandemic

The pandemic was in full force! A time of social, civil, and racial unrest. I thought I found myself alone. The thing is, I wasn't alone. The isolation from the pandemic caused me to get into the presence of God.

I was not living up to my full potential. I was considering moving back to Chicago after having separation anxiety when my "Big Babies" relocated back to Chicago with MyPinky, missing our meditation time we shared.

I was grateful that I now had a place of work. I started with the Post Office after sitting on my ASSest for two years to secure the bag. In my denial of fear, shame, and guilt, pride held me from disclosing that I fell backward inside my truck over a bin, imbalanced from my elbow surgery. This happened right when I was returning to work. I continued working through the day, feeling the effects from previous knee injuries. So much for "Chasing a bag."

Healing from a lower back sprain, torn hip, buttock, IT Band, right knee, and ankle sprain, I was self-quarantined (isolation), unable to physically go to therapy due to underlying issues, putting myself at risk of contracting COVID-19, not eating clean, gaining 15lbs during the quarantine and I was typically away from my family and displaying signs of depression that would've gone ignored.

I began Reiki meditation under the guidance of a dear 'Sister Friend,' experiencing an awakening. Awakening is the realization that the swirling flakes are just swirling flakes. In other words, the movements of the mind are just movements of the mind. The mind can be chaotic, or the mind can be peaceful. The emotions can be positive or negative, highly active or peaceful. Awakening is the understanding that you are not your thoughts and feelings at all.

Maybe the Journey isn't so much about becoming anything. Maybe it's about un-becoming everything that isn't you, so you can be who you were meant to be in the first place.

Unknown

THE NEED

No Excuses, Make It Happen

So... I'm in all this pain, and the doctors are telling me that my hip is not torn. A bone-like cyst was found on the arthrogram after a tear was seen on the MRI previously taken at a facility called Prime Imaging. Being my own health advocate, I made an appointment to see my Primary Care Physician (PCP), thinking this was the cause of the continuous pain. He then referred me to a sarcoma orthopedic, where a pelvic X-ray was taken and compared to the other images. This confirmed a labrum tear in my right hip, which was suspected on the first MRI.

While having a complete exam with my PCP, I was being diagnosed with Leukopenia. Leukopenia is when a reduced number of white blood cells is in the peripheral blood. A smear is essential for determining which white cell line is responsible for decreasing the total white cell count. It should be examined for the presence of abnormal forms. The presence of immature ("left-shifted") white cells can indicate infection or malignancy myelodysplasia or acute leukemia. Meanwhile, abnormal red cells can indicate the presence of autoimmune destruction, myelodysp- lasia or bone marrow failure syndrome. Further testing should be guided by the type of deficient cells and the features of the presentation- Christopher Gibson Nancy Berliner Hematology Leukopenia.

My PCP put me on a medically supervised weight management program. I lost 6lbs. *Be as Fearless as the Women you admire* is what kept going through my head. I got my Prayer Warrior Sisters to agree with me for the simplest causation for treatment. I had a bone marrow aspirate and biopsy done. Prior to the procedure, I saw the pain specialist doctor from the Department of Labor (DOL).

No Sleep

Fear of going to sleep, I was awake for three days, putting the pages of my story together. I had been prescribed seven pills, of which I only had four left. Me and MyGoodJudy, which is my son's God mother, were being challenged in our health. We received our biopsy reports on the same dates. Her tumor was Benign, my favorite B-word. I was grateful, expressing to her that the "S" couldn't do this without "T". In high school, that's what we called ourselves, the "S" and the "T". My bone marrow came back good; no further treatment was needed at that time. I had to begin keeping watch of my blood levels.

I took a Tylenol with codeine to alleviate the pain after having both my knees injected a couple of days before and after the bone marrow procedure.

It was the hottest month in Texas, yet I was cold. I didn't have the air conditioning, nor fan was on. My back was hurting me badly. My knees were swollen. I took the Tylenol three and blacked out again.

After sharing with MyGoodJudy that I had seven Tylenol, I stated, "there were only four left in the bottle."

"You'll be fine," she said.

I went on sharing with MyGoodJudy how I thought I missed MyBestie's birthday. I told her that Bestie did not say anything during our conversation after I expressed to her that I was feeling foggy again. My Bestie and I were on Facetime, and I turned the camera around to show her all of my journals, notes, notepads, pens &

A SOUND MIND

pencils. I had so many pages written down, and they were all spread out across the floor. She had gifted me a pink rose gold journal with the words "Make It Happen" written on the cover with a pink fluffy ink pen and a decorative box with words of affirmation on it reading: "You've got this" "Do more Awesome" "stay YOU."

After sharing this with MyGoodJudy, I stated, "I'm going to just shut my ugly ace up (*insider*)." Can't nobody say *ugly ass* like MyGoodJudy.

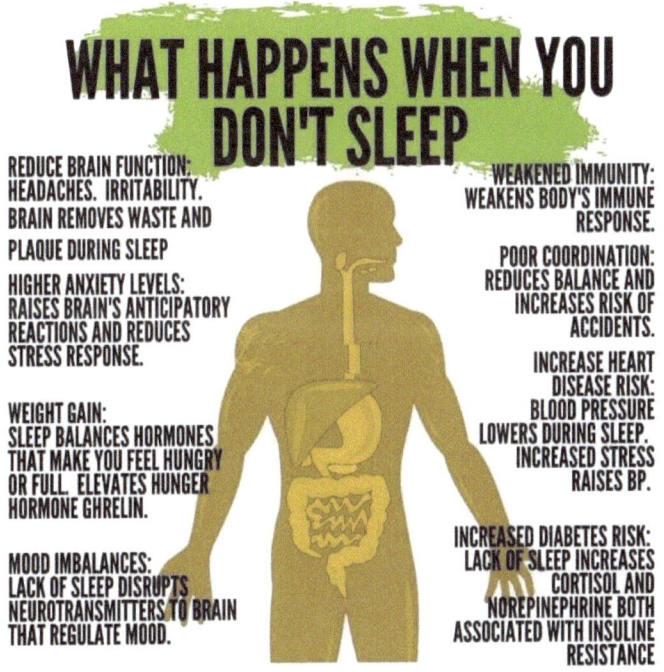

Again, fearful of me going to sleep, I called my only LIVING Sultry-Sexy-Sensational-Aunt, to say Happy Birthday, and tell her that I completed my book. In one of our many previous conversations, I mentioned that I had been writing.

"Stacie, you should write. You have a way with the words," she would say.

"I have a great appreciation for acronyms," I said. We laughed. I continued by saying, "On your day, designed with you in mind, A Sound Mind, the Rebirth was birthed."

Prayer of Focus

God, my singular ambition in life is to magnify your Son; I don't care how you fit me into your plan; send me as you please. I place no conditions on your arrangement. You set the term of my service. My only prayer is that you ordain my life. Whatever glorifies Christ most through me. If my savior is honored more by my death than my life, more in sickness than in health, more through loneliness than companionship, more by the appearance of failure than by the trapping of success, more by anonymity than notoriety. In that case, your design is my desire only to let me make a difference.

"Our deepest fear is not that we are inadequate. Our deepest fear is that we are powerful beyond measure. It is our light, not our darkness that most frightens us. We ask ourselves, Who am I to be brilliant, gorgeous, talented, fabulous? Actually, who are you not to be? You are a child of God. Your playing small does not serve the world. There is nothing enlightened about shrinking so that other people won't feel insecure around you. We are all meant to shine, as children do. We were born to make manifest the glory of God that is within us. It's not just in some of us; it's in everyone. And as we let our own light shine, we unconsciously give other people permission to do the same. As we are liberated from our own fear, our presence automatically liberates others."

- Marianne Williamson

kiwi-ol.tumblr.com

PROCEDURE ON MY RIGHT HIP

I was cleared to have a less invasive procedure on my right hip in December 2020, staying in compliance with the Postal Service Department of Labor regulations. I still had two more procedures to be done as long as my leukopenia labs continued to read mild. I knew my healing journey was going to be lengthy. I decided that I would heal at ThePinkPalace. That's what I call my apartment, my space. Everything was pre-prepped, even my holiday decor. I was prepared for my healing journey holistically to begin.

Two out of the four CEOs of my company Wakanna prayed for me before my procedure. I didn't take for granted that it was the visionary Pillar of Legacy and The Midwife, the Pillar of Wealth, who birth possibilities, which I had the opportunity to meet in person. We greeted with an elbow bump.

The Powerful voice I heard was the Pillar of Freedom, giving words of encouragement. The CFO freed my heart. Pillar of Health. The CMO explained the science, correcting me mixing the tinctures, recommending our HempraniumMD Pillar of Health.

Seeing the open platform and opportunity to share my two-part story on how the two epic, failed experiences intertwined. This is what brought me to WakannaWhy.

God places you right where you need to be with the people you need to be around. I believe in divine order. When I read MomD's testimony. MomD is a mother figure in my business. She shared how the WaKanna Cannabidiol (CBD) products helped her avoid hip surgery and presented some similar issues as I was challenged with. Looking for a more natural holistic approach towards my healing journey, I reached out to her. After she went on to share the information about the products with me, I was impressed with the presentation and the videos. It was a radio talk interview for me. I was listening to four women who look like me, creating a space I could relate to.

I remembered the conversation with Mr. Diamond via messenger. He's a friend I went to high school with. We call him Mr. Diamond because that's a rank in the business of WaKanna.

He asked the question about a year ago. "What's the hottest thing on the market right now?"

I replied, "Lashes."

Oh, so this is what Mr. Diamond was talking about. MomD had stated that Mr. Diamond was the orchestrator in the business, that she wasn't involved as much as she was with a previous business we were in together. I stated to her that I didn't want to team up with Mr. Diamond again. Listen to how faith works. The first 'Wake Up Wealthy' call I was on woke me up! A Powerful voice spoke to my heart. After the call, I shook my globe. I got out of my own way and phoned MomD. When she answered my call, I said, Crown Me! We did a three-way call with Mr. Diamond. This was BIGGER THAN US!

Now, there was no disrespect for not putting the title 'Minister' in front of Mr. Diamond's name. I didn't meet him as a Minister, as I watched him humble himself after earning that title in the company. As he stretched out his arm with a key in his hand, passing the baton, My Brother was ministering, which symbolized to me a gift of life. I received that gift and more; he had spoken into my life when I made my transformation and relocated to Texas.

Mr. Diamond stated, "Stacie, you are such a testimony and inspiration to so many people. I mean, it wasn't a cake walk, but we worked as a team to get it done. I do praise God for (two other ladies) If those two wouldn't have said Mooney let's do this, and we with you. I know that you, I,

A SOUND MIND

and many others wouldn't know this mean of impacting many all those that will receive Stacie, you are a Texan Star!"

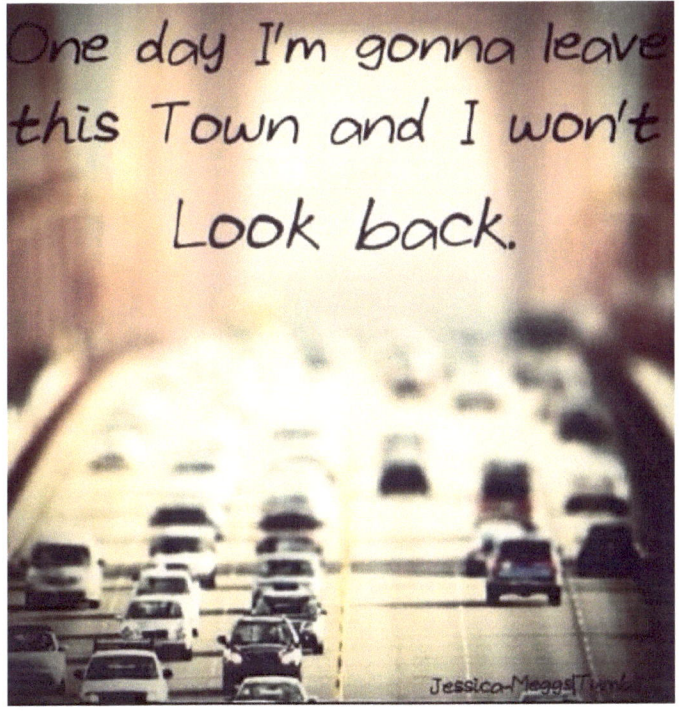

Words Have Power

I would always state that if I smoked marijuana, that I would die, and I died! And you ask, "*how did you die Stacie?* Well, I died 76 times, repeating the same story, trying to change the ending to avoid dying. This is how it happened. I went on a 3-day "field trip" for each brownie that I ate. And you ask, "*how many brownies did you eat, Stacie?*" I ate three brownies with marijuana! This was the inner fat girl in me. I knew they were "special brownies" after eating the first one and didn't feel anything, thinking they were just Godiva Carmel with nuts brownies.

When the weed (THC) kicked in, OOO WEEE... It was Show-Time! I lived my life out loud, literally. Well, that's how I expected my life to be when I relocated to Texas in December 2014, until the present. That's why I am like Smokey in the movie Friday, *FORK GETTING HIGH!* That was the first and the last for me. That's how we got here.

"Our expectations yield a tremendous power in our lives. We don't always get what we deserve in life, but we usually always get no more than expected. We receive what we believe. Unfortunately, this principle works as strongly in the negative as it does in the positive. Many people expect defeat, failure, and mediocrity, and they usually get it. You can also believe in good things just as easily as you can expect the worst. When you encounter tough times, ask for wisdom, change what you expect. Even if the bottom falls out of your life, your attitude should be: I know that you're going to use this for my good. I believe that you're going to bring me out stronger than before."

Shaking my glove, I then texted MyLifePartner:

Idk what God is doing in my life, But HE knows... I came to Texas five years ago to grow my business. You stated that "You were about to put Rowlett on the map." Get ready for the BLOOM! Don't be afraid to start over; we're starting with experience. Let's LIVE LifePartner! Get the ring so that you can love me like The Notebook. I love you ♡

THE GIFT

Where It All Comes Together

We tend to think of God's given gifts as these things pertaining to the church. Well, guess what, you are the church! Gifts are more than just financial or material resources. Your gift might be a skill you have developed or expert knowledge you gained. It might be the time you have on your hands. It could be the gift of your smile or a few encouraging words. It could be the gift of your presence. You may not know what your gift is, and it's okay. Have your eyes and heart open when you approach the world with a readiness to hear from God, an openness to the voice of the Holy Spirit. Eventually, the universe will speak to you.

A SOUND MIND

The Cleanse

After I discontinued taking all pills, including the weight loss ones, my doctor prescribed, my body was attacking itself. I was flushing out my system naturally by using WaKanna products, Bitters /Belly Brew coffee, making a mixture of all of our tinctures that you can ingest, taking the maximum drops (15) daily for overall health. I also took 1 Broad Spectrum Gummy midday, replacing ibuprofen. I made a mixture of tea tree oil, peppermint oil, Dr. Rita's rub, and the pain relief cream, and now, I have little to no scarring. I vamped throughout the day for clarity. 1/2 Power gummy at night along with my tincture helps with restful nights, REM sleep (hot flashes), staying asleep, waking rested. On Royal soak nights, I soak with our CBD bath soak and OUD oil to relieve some of the inflammation.

I took daily showers and moisturized my skin with our mango CBD lotion. I mixed it with Glow Naked OUD oil. I moisture my face with our CBD face serum Wholly Glow. I promise I feel like I had an instant facelift. I used one drop of Essential Defense with peppermint oil. It became my new mouthwash. I have mixed up a spray bottle with our leave-in conditioner and HempPowerHair oil to spray on my scalp to help grow my edges of my hair in. I also season my meals with our flavorful seasonings and butter. In addition, I light my candle and sip my Essential Defense tea with a spoonful of Honeybee. I became a product of the products feeding my receptors. There are ten receptors that crave Cannabidiol (CBD) to maintain homeostasis. CBD brought my body back into balance. I was able to have the health without the high. "A Sound Mind"- finding balance is all about what works in your life. Most people try to turn back their odometers. I want people to know why I look this way. I've traveled a long way, and some of the roads weren't paved.

A SOUND MIND

~Albert Einstein

Manifest

God put dreams on your hearts bigger than you so that you rely on Him and His Power.

Tony Evans

God heard your prayer. God sees your situation, your blessing, your healing, your answer is coming.

July of 2020, I asked the universe to surprise me.

A memory of a text message from 2015 came up:

Lady Des: Stacie, do you have a published book?

Me: Lady Des! No, I don't, not yet ☺. I receive that.

Lady Des: Yes, as I read this post, I seriously heard/sensed you writing books and publishing. Although I don't know your voice, I perceive you have the voice of a writer.

Me: Lady Des, with my hands raised high, let me stop procrastinating! Most people say I have a pleasant phone voice.

Lady Des: To God be the Glory!

Me: All the Glory be to God!

I thought to myself, *Wow! Save that to your phone.* To this day, I don't know what post we were referring to. The universe did.

A SOUND MIND

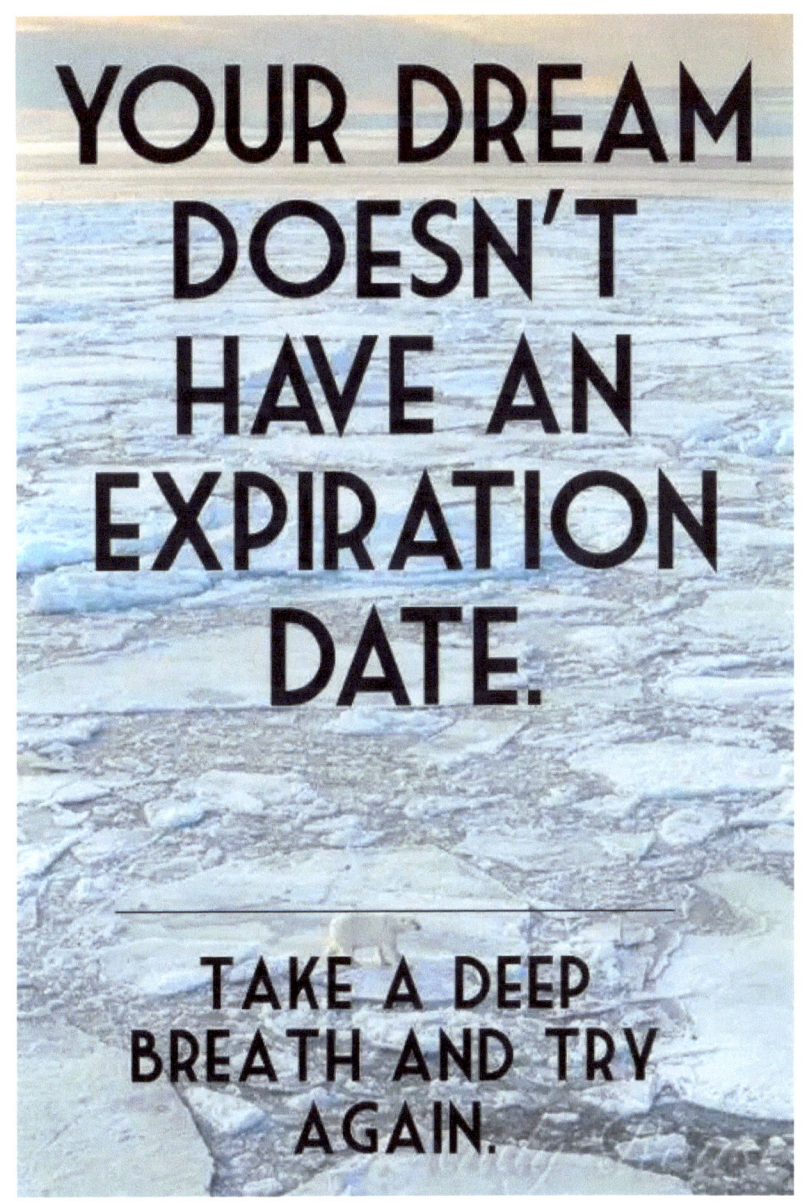

After reading The Adventure backward, how I had written it, spilling all the tea, mixing the two experiences, trying to avoid 'The Journey' and 'The Gift' colliding, the miscarriage of the unfinished manuscript was sent out too early. Every 10th page in the journal was an encouragement, some knowingly and unknowingly spoken words into my life. It was reminding me of why I was writing My Story in the first place. *Order my steps* are the words tattooed on my left foot.

ME, AFTER TRUSTING IN GOD AND ALLOWING HIM TO ORDER MY STEPS.

A SOUND MIND

Some highways lead to the center of your purpose. The roads of experience, opportunities, passions, and abilities are all designed to lead you to the intersection of your purpose in God and your calling for your life here on earth.

I reached out to Authoress Sylvia via text:

"Glad Morning Beautiful! This is Stacie. I reset my phone and lost our text. If I'm going to quote you, I want to quote you correctly. Do you remember stating 'how some things won't have anything to do with the book?' I need those words of confirmation, Sister.

"God, Morning beautiful!" replied Authoress. I will forward the text.

Forwarded text: *...and there will be times, you hear God's voice, but feel it has nothing to do with your book. Write those moments down, for they may be for the book but not at that moment. "*

There's no table of content in the book of life. You don't know if you're at the beginning or the ending of your story, so make sure when you turn the page to your next chapter. You approach it with Gratitude for what you have in the midst of getting what you want.

Khalilah, my DJ VA's wife, started sharing on manifesting, which I had begun tapping into. This resonated with me.

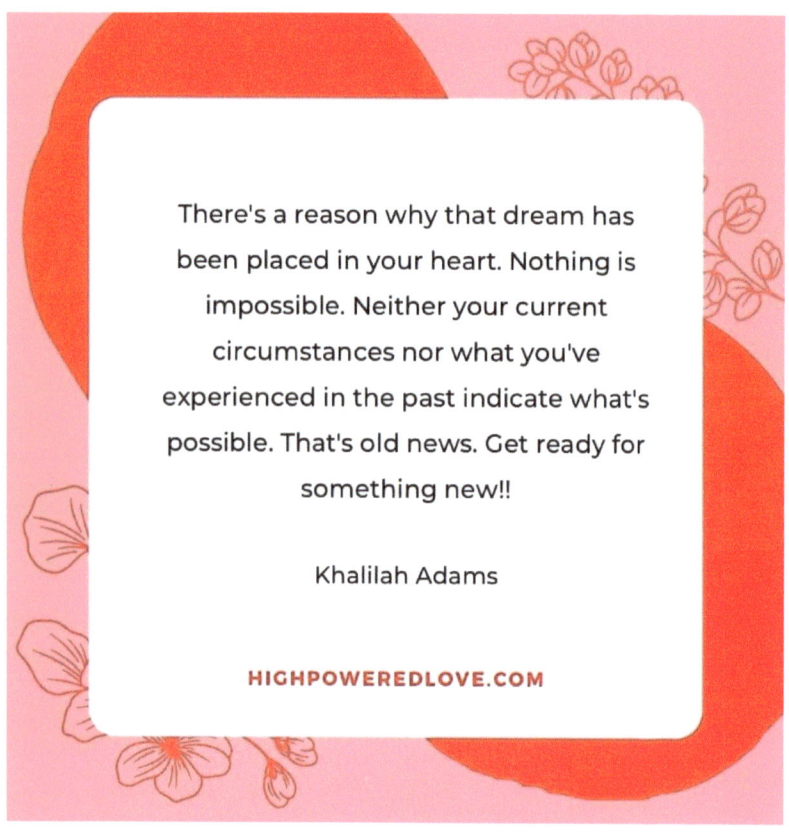

The purpose of life is to discover your gift. The work of life is to develop it. The meaning of life is to give it away- David Viscott

My Little Sister's book was released. Faith knew

that I was going to read her story. The book went to apt 224 on the other side of the complex, my candle-making kit, and some other items. everything that was going to keep me from writing My Story was trying to keep myself busy

B eing
U nder
S atans
Y olk

Acronym for BUSY my BigSisterPrayerWarrior came up with. No more distractions. They were intercepted. I relate everything to Football. I did get refunded for the items, just in case you're reading this and wondering.

My Cousin had gifted me a Black quartz crystal. It's used when you need protection mental fortitude, operating on a different frequency. How are you coming out of this pandemic, or something related to it was down my timeline?

STACIE CALVIN

CORONA

- Calm-Stay
- Organize- organize your thoughts
- Rest- rest up while you can
- Organize- organize your life
- Navigate- navigate your way through this
- Accomplish- accomplish what you set out to do

2020 Vision, write the vision and make it plan
The vision is the place you go to see the future.
See it before you see it.

When you focus on problems:

P redictions
R eminders
O pportunities
B lessings
L essons
E verywhere
M essages
S olvable

You'll have more problems. When you focus on possibilities, you'll have more opportunities.

A SOUND MIND

Opportunity knocks this perfect time for manifesting your thoughts into reality Focus on what you want, not on what you don't want—the opening of the vortex.

It says you are in alignment—the right time to manifest. Connect within to find answers. You are connected to the source. Reap your rewards. Your energy work has opened this portal for you Align and Reap Your Rewards.

I reached out to give an update:

Greetings, Beautiful just wanted to check in to let you know the writing journey continues. It is written Still trusting and believing God for some things to come to pass.

"Greetings, Beautiful! Please don't waste another day worrying about how to finance it. It's not hard or expensive. I do want to encourage you to set aside time to "Write" This is the best time, finish 2020 strong!"

Received!!! "Amen"

THE JOY

Excellence & Beauty at Its Best

I witnessed a historical moment in 2009, the First Black President of the U.S. was sworn in. On Wednesday, January 20, 2021, I witnessed another inspiring moment, the First Black Woman was sworn in as Vice President with her *Chucks and Pearls* theme. Chucks became my signature shoe after my many injuries. I could no longer wear my signature heels, revealing my height of 5'2" with shoes on.

There was nothing that I couldn't do! I wasn't going to allow anything to take away that Wonderful Wednesday event, Not Even ME! Going into Black History Month, I was so empowered that I felt like I was standing 6'1"!

A 90-day 15k Wealth Massive Action Pledge was called. In preparation, there were questions asked, to which I answered the pledge based on my story. I had to finish the task! The finishing is connected to My Legacy, adding a 90-day Wellness journey.

> The Game Plan and Opportunity

I reached out to our CEO of WaKanna and notified her that I would email her the Synopsis and *The Joy*, the last chapter of my story. I asked her if she would edit my story written in my journal when I came home to Chicago. I expressed that I would like to shadow her while I was there for a day or two. I began to think to myself; *I'm not sure if this is how the story ends because it's not finished. I have more. Maybe I should wait until these things come to pass within the next 90 days.* I was going back and forth, answering my own questions. Shaking my globe...

One of my favorite quotes from Oprah Winfrey is *We get in Life What we have the Courage to ask for.*

WaKanna Wellness Health Conference 2021 was Awwmazing and all in alignment. I shared with MomD, my mother figure of WaKanna, everything that was going on with me in my personal life. I expressed to her how I felt about not having a team, and the email I sent to our CEO of WaKanna about the final chapter of my story, hoping she did not receive it. I told MomD I needed to press the reset button or take a different approach, starting Feb 1st., to building my WaKanna business. I explained to her that I was not capable of leading from the front, that my son was suffering daily living with depression, and how I am not able to help him. I'm just everybody's cheerleader!

MomD was strategizing with me to help me reach my goal. You gotta love her. She suggested that I start looking for vending events and things that were going on in my community.

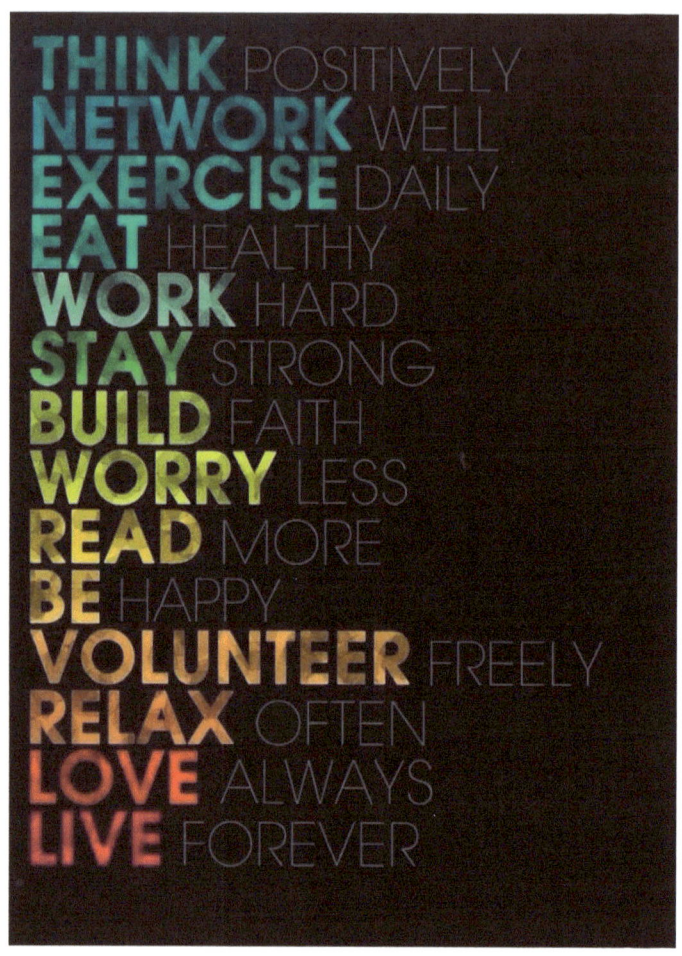

I began to use my networking resources. I joined a new group on Social Media daily, adding new friends. A vending event opportunity was eventually presented.

When asked what is that I sold, I answered, "WaKanna's Anxiety Relief Products."

"CBD! Omg, yes, I was looking for someone," responded the host of the event. She continued to say that she wanted an older representative and one who could be able to explain the difference between CBD and marijuana."

"I'm here," I said. "That's what we do. We educate! "

While awaiting further notification of the event, I continued my education on CBD vs. Marijuana through WaKanna University. The vending event was eventually postponed because there was a change in the weather, a State of an Emergency power outage, and no heat or running water in most cities of Texas where the event would be held. In short, this was a disaster! Guess who wasn't affected? You guessed correctly, Not I!

Although we were still advised to boil our water and keep the faucets dripping.

My Life Partner had come over to ThePinkPalace. "The land of free-flowing water and heat" is how he described his whereabouts with his sisters after being without water and heat. I referenced that to God, keeping his promises in John 7. God promised whoever believes in him that rivers of living water will flow from within.

The Significance of the Numbers

THE NUMBER 7 symbolizes every positive and valuable matter in existence like prosperous life, happiness, renewal and perfection. It means complete. My therapist had given me Luke 7 to read. He said to me, "Go in peace."

THE NUMBER 3 was significant throughout my journey. Three, spiritually, is a Holy Number. It represents the Holy Trinity that makes up three divine beings, God the Father, God the Son and God the Holy Spirit. Do not give up on anything that you do, since the angels are with you. Keep on praying and meditating, and surely blessings will be upon you. This number will help you focus on your spiritual life.

A SOUND MIND

THE NUMBER 5 is a symbol of balance. It means that you have to keep a balance between material and spiritual aspects in your life. We can say that angel number 5 is also a symbol of individualism, courage and meaningful life lessons you have learned through your own experience.

THE NUMBER 15, its priorities are family, harmony and health. There is an urge for everything to be ideal. The ideal 15 has evolved as its own. There is responsibility, love, self-sacrifice, protection of family members, sympathy and compassion.

THE NUMBER 25 represents change. Whether this change will be a professional one or a personal one, you have yet to see. Seeing this number frequently in your life brings you to a period of big decisions. The decisions are going to cause change that is extremely necessary for your life. It brings you a new sense of self. You will take actions more seriously, and you will almost grow overnight. Life won't be the same after this; it is a natural course we all have to take. Don't get overwhelmed by these changes. Try to embrace them with an open heart. Sometimes even though we don't want things to change, we are clueless about possibilities that we are missing out on by staying in the same spot, pressuring things bound to fail. It may bring a lot of sadness because not all of us can adapt to change quickly. People leaving our lives and situations that are going to be challenging can leave us feeling broken. This necessary step in your life will shape your character and make you the person you are supposed to be.

THE NUMBER 30 will help you express yourself and use your natural abilities. Thanks to this number, you will realize that a certain cycle in your life has to end because another process will begin soon.

THE NUMBER 76 calls on you to think of the adversities you've overcome in the past. You've had to display lots of courage to achieve what you have managed to. This is the same courage you are being called upon to exude moving forward. In addition, number 76 signifies confidence. Your angels are asking you to have faith in your skills and abilities. Trust that you have the necessary resources to manifest the desires of your heart.

ANGEL NUMBER 116 comes to you to show that this is the time to aim higher in order to achieve all your goals and make your dreams come true. Your guardian angel will not see you toil and fail to reward you. To the hard workers, this number is a sign that your efforts are being recognized, and your future will be bright. One by one, your

A SOUND MIND

dreams will come true with the help and guidance of your angels. You only need to believe and trust in God to make a way for you where there seems to be no way. Do not give up on your dreams because even God has not given up on us, although we are sinners and have fallen short of His glory. Blessings will come your way, and you are obligated to enjoy them because you have worked for the same. *The number of pages in my book is 116.*

(reference: sunsigns.org)

It's Already Written

When God says that He works from the end to the beginning, He says that He has already completed the blueprint in the spiritual realm for what you are to do in the physical realm. He knows your destiny. His goals for you are already made. His desires for you have already been determined. He has already dreamed His dream for you. What He is doing now is simply rolling back through time to seek out your cooperation to begin walking in what He has already prepared for you to do.

1 Chronicles 4:10 NLT
Make Room, GOD Is ENLARGING your territory.

The shift began on Valentine's weekend. I saw things from a different perspective, thanks to a neighbor.

"Letting someone create a false narrative of you is a small price to pay for having rid yourself of their toxicity. Let them say what they want; if you and the highest know the truth, your life will flourish, and their lies will rot theirs."

Don't let the darkness from your past block the light of joy in your present. What happened is done. Stop giving time to things that no longer exist when there is so much joy to be found here and now.

-Karen Salmansohn

Healing & Finding My Joy

I Choose Joy! Why?
The Joy of The Lord Is My Strength.

"Strength" leaves us feeling as if we have to do everything for ourselves and by ourselves. This thinking leaves us with an incomplete energetic circuit carrying an unbearable physical, mental and emotional load. Under these conditions, you will most certainly break.

"Strength" is NOT in our individuality. That's where creativity lives. Strength lives in our collective engagement. Like the roots of a tree, strength is produced by communing with others. If you want true strength, connect and participate in a healthy village (i.e., friends, family, community, etc.). Your ability to engage in a healthy reciprocal relationship is where your TRUE strength is cultivated. You were not made to do this alone! Stop judging yourself, stop judging others and instead, share the load. Many hands make light work. If you were not born into a strong village, make it your mission to build one. There, you will find your true strength. "

What is important to you? Forgive. This is one of the most critical components of healing, to forgive yourself, others, and life. To forgive what has been, what is and what is playing out in the world. Meditate on this; find what you have not let go of and release the need to hold onto that which does not serve you anymore.

I was prepared to heal at ThePinkPalace. My wellness tray and other personal items all within reach, the procedure went well. It was recommended for me not to go up the stairs, so I recovered at MyLifePartner's house. While recovering, I experienced an allergic reaction to anesthesia. My lip and ears were numb, and my throat sore and swollen. It hurt to clear my throat, and my chest and back felt broken. I couldn't sit up; every movement was painful. I was refusing to take anything other than my products because my body composition with anesthesia and opioids don't mix. I took two Benadryl tablets, one every four hours. After speaking with the surgeon coordinator, I fell asleep after vaping and after 1/2 power gummy.

Mid-Morning the next day, MyLifePartner rubbed me down with extreme pain cream and OUD oil. He laid me back on the heating pad after drinking some broth and taking my tincture. Tincture is CBD oil that is placed under your tongue. You hold it for 60 seconds, and it gets into your blood stream quicker. I vaped, and I took 1broadspectrum gummy without THC. It has numerous health benefits. I was relaxed, and I slept until he returned home.

As I awakened, it was still challenging to sit up. I phoned the Department of Labor (DOL) nurse assigned to me for my elbow surgery, stating my symptoms, making her aware that I was not taking any pain medication. The nurse was impressed. Her recommendation was for me to go to the ER to check if it was something treatable.

Several tests were taken, including the COVID-19 test. I drank WaKanna detox tea 24 hours before the surgery, so my potassium being low was understandable. All the other tests came back negative. Liver enzymes were low, which is rare. The Doctor suggested that I redo both tests with my PCP. The follow-up appointment with the surgeon suggested I follow up regarding the soreness and numbness that I was still experiencing, "See you in four weeks" As I arrived back at MyLifePartner' s house, my knee was hot to touch, tight and swollen, looking about ready to burst, I needed ICE:

- **I** ce
- **C** ompression
- **E** levate

I broke down and took one tramadol, which was one of the two prescriptions prescribed for both muscle relaxers. I was apprehensive about taking. I didn't want my facial muscles to relax in the way they were.

Laying on his couch triggered me. I panicked! All I had with me was my vape pen. The immediate reaction was precisely what was needed and to get back to ThePinkPalace.

On my employee ID, the expiration date is 4/2022. After three surgeries, all with complications, allergic reactions, and infections, this led me to write a letter resigning from the Post Office. All things are possible. I was scheduled for a therapy session and was given an assignment; a chart asking *what need is needed*? My eyes locked to the top of the pyramid Self-actualization -Self-fulfillment, achieving one's full potential, including creative activities.

"You cannot afford to live in potential for the rest of your life; at some point, you have to unleash the potential and make your move."

Eric T.

Prayer of focus

Please help me stand for what I know is right and not waver under pressure from the world. Don't let me be a woman who is "always learning and never able to come to a knowledge of the truth." Give me a teachable spirit that is willing to listen to the voice of wisdom and grow in Your ways.

What are you doing for your business is another question asked from the WaKanna Massive Action Challenge? *Reintroduce myself; turn my adversity into ambition. Re-establish my relationship with wealth. Being Rich not monetarily, although I'm walking in my wealthy place.*

Dr. Erica acronym for **RICH:**

R ecognize
I dentify
C hange
H eal

Proverbs 28:6 KJV
Better is the poor who walks in his integrity than one perverse in his ways, though he is rich.

I am My Most Valued Asset in My Life. Having this time led me to my passion, and passion is energy. Pay attention to the things that naturally energize you. Follow the energy. As you journey this path called destiny, remember always to stay hooked up to the engine of God so that He can take you where you need to go.

Staying stagnant mentally, emotionally, spiritually, and physically was not an option for me to BE my best version of myself. I was preparing for my left knee to be scoped in March, knowing that my mobility would be limited. They say abs are made in the kitchen. This Wellness Journey, much like my transformation, wasn't for a physical appearance. *My Health is My Wealth*!

4 a.m. was known as my see into me time; my intimacy time with God. 4 a.m. become mediation, writing, and sipping tea time. 5 a.m. was my workout time known on Facebook during my transformation. 6 a.m. I would usually take a nap, wake with WaKanna daily 8 a.m. call, walk on my waver machine for 30 minutes, and I create my day.

I'm so happy and grateful that I enhanced my nutrition knowledge while approaching my wellness journey, focusing on my physical, spiritual, mental, and career goals. Through WaKanna, I was helping women and men with digestive issues, fatigue, and hormonal imbalance to achieve their optimal wellness. I lived with digestive distress throughout my teenage years and half of my adult life. Our Wholey Herb- Wholey diet (which I don't use the word diet, the first three letters spell die)- I'm not dying! I've reclaimed my physical body as my own and am regrading myself as a Temple, a vessel of divine light.

April 20th is "weed day." That day is WaKanna's 2nd anniversary of our Wealth and Freedom Conference. *Writing this book is the beginning of my freedom.*

A SOUND MIND

> Galatians 5:13 NLT
> *For you have been called to live in freedom, my brothers and sisters. But don't use your freedom to satisfy your sinful nature. Instead, use your freedom to serve one another in love.*

The Symbolism of Trees

WAKANNA® was brought into existence through the synergistic efforts and shared foundational values of four African-American women who believe health, wealth, legacy, and freedom are gifts that belong to all people. WaKanna core values Empower, Equality, Trust, Respect, and Excellence.

WAKANNA meaning:
Females (Girls)
Leaves (Young)
Gift of God
Total Harmony

A Wakannaperneuer is what we in WaKanna Nation call ourselves, instead of entrepreneurs.

I launched TLK Dispensary Wellness Solutions (FlywithPinky), my signature Eucalyptus oil tea light candles, signature Immune Defense, boosted tea bombs.

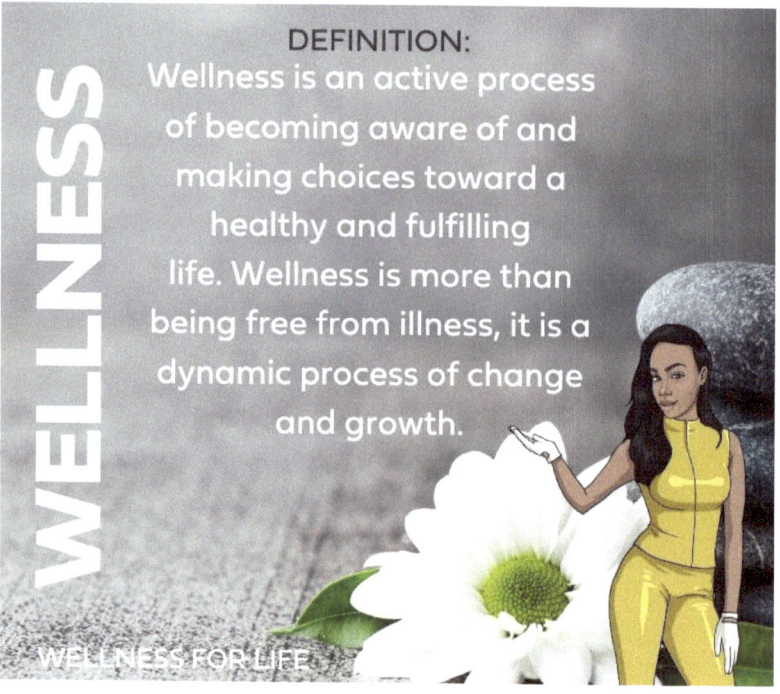

My theme for the holidays was Trees, and the display was left out intentionally. Trees symbolize togetherness and serve as a reminder that you are never alone or isolated.

Trees are a universal symbol of strength and growth as they stand tall and strong all over the world. They spread their roots deep into the soil and stabilize themselves. Trees can weather the toughest of storms, which is why they are such a prominent symbol of strength. The Tree of Life represents growth, as a tree starts as a small, delicate sapling and grows into a giant, strong tree over a long time. The tree grows up and outwards, representing how a person grows stronger and increases their knowledge and experiences throughout their lifetime.

The Tree of Life symbolizes individuality; trees are all unique, with their branches sprouting at different points and in different directions. A tree symbolizes a person's personal growth into a unique human being as different experiences shape them into who they are. Over time, trees gain more distinctive characteristics; as branches break off, new ones grow, and as the weather takes its toll - the tree remains solid and sturdy. This is a metaphor for how people grow and change throughout their lifetime and how their unique experiences mold them and enhance their individuality.

In addition, the Tree of Life symbolizes rebirth, as trees lose their leaves and seem to be dead during winter, but new buds appear, and new, fresh leaves unfurl during the spring. This represents the beginning of a new life and a fresh start. The Tree of Life also symbolizes immortality because even as the tree grows old, it creates seeds that carry its essence, so it lives on through new saplings.

Trees have always evoked a sense of calm and peace, so it is unsurprising that the Tree of Life is also a symbol of peacefulness and relaxation. Not having the urge to explain yourself is real peace. Trees have a relaxing presence, as they stand tall and still while their leaves flutter in the breeze. The Tree of Life serves as a reminder for the unique, calming feeling that one gets from trees.

One of the last questions from the WaKanna Massive Action Challenge asked was, "What would you do if you had a billion dollars and all the time in the world?" *Invest in the people that invest in you. Invest in your dream. Grind now. Shine later.*

A SOUND MIND

April showers bring May flowers.

I was turning 50 Full Bloom! 18 with 32 years of experience. I had my son at 18, my first, most life-changing, challenging gift. He turns 32 on May 22. After 50 plus, we should be blooming beautifully and enjoying the fruits of life with nurturing and positive growth.

Snow Globe Metaphor

I love the metaphor, *"mediation is like a snow globe."* When you shake the globe, the sand and water get stirred up, making the water cloudy. When the globe is left undisturbed, the sand settles, and the water becomes clear again. If you think about it, our mind is like the sand and water when it's shaken up: thoughts flying everywhere in a chaotic swirl, but the mediative mind is supposed to be like a snow globe when the flakes all settle. Practicing mindfulness can help us to become aware of this process, letting the snowflakes gradually settle, creating some space between our thoughts, emotions, and reactions. Often, I find a real prejudice against thinking in the meditation community. Thoughts are bad. Thoughts should stop. Thoughts are wrong. My mind is a "monkey mind," and I cannot have peace while it is jumping about.

I understand this viewpoint, but I think it is partaking of a deep conditionality, a grasping, if you will, after a still mind. If you cannot accept reality without a still mind, then you cannot accept reality.

Engaging the mind just the way it is, is a powerful way to unleash your creativity, as well as take steps towards resolving long-held psychological difficulties. You can begin to experience the mind as it is—a natural flow of thoughts and images that have the quality, appropriately enough, of the sky, the clouds, the wind, and the weather. Beautiful and wild. So, when life shakes your snow globe, let the snowflakes fly!"

We are like a snowflake, all different in our own beautiful way. God created each one of us in our unique way. Just like a snowflake, we all have a blueprint that differs from one another.

Eph 2:10 NLT
For we are God's masterpiece. He has created us anew in Christ Jesus, so we can do the good things He planned for us long ago.

My Bucket List from 2014-2016

Checking Off Things on My
Live List by 50

Stand for election ✔
Reunite with an old friend ✔
Travel to Hawaii ✔
Be in great health ✔
Write a best-selling book ✔

> Don't forget you can
> Start at 40
> Fail at 45
> Start again at 46
> Not be great
> Not get better
> Be different from anyone else
> Find your lane
> Pick the wrong circle
> Go after the wrong business
> Find the right business
> Start again at 50
> ...and still, succeed

I made my request known that by fifty I wanted to own some Things MANIFESTING!!! This was preparation. I got distracted, made some mistakes, broke some promises, and forgot who I was. I lost my mind and took on the mind of Christ. *"The Rebirth."*

Promise Keeper

March 25, 2021, I sign my publishing package (the end of the month) for the launch of A Sound Mind-The Rebirth (May 25 my 50th Birthday.) April showers bring May flowers.

Full Bloom! 18 with 32 years of experience. I had my son at 18, my first most life-changing challenging gift. He turns 32 May 22, after the age of 50 plus. We should be blooming beautifully and enjoying the fruits of life with nurturing and positive growth. Every 25 days out of 90 days. Something came to pass. So many opportunities are being birthed. Partnering with S.H.E PUBLISHING LLC Sister company S.H.E-SASSY Publishing LLC

My vision wall came to fruition. My unique gift crash- ed into the world's need. Health Life Prosperity collides with Health Wealth Legacy Freedom, health without the high. In these times, we need to know all the tools available to assist in us coping with depress- ion and anxiety that has plagued so many of us. The opioid epidemic is at an all-time high. There are better alternatives for your peace.

My favorite passage:

Be still and know that I am God psalm 46:10

Be Still...stop talking, switch off the phone, stop commenting Listen, stop arguing, stop questioning stop moaning

and know...stop doubting Be sure Have faith no second opinion

I am God
God Is Almighty
God Is in control
God Is love
God Is King
God Is my hope, rock, fortress
God Is ever-present, a help in times of trouble
God Is my shepherd
He will lead me, nourish me, protect me and restore me.

A SOUND MIND

Sometimes it takes ten years to get to that one year that will change your life. Keep going.

STACIE CALVIN

A SOUND MIND

Synopsis

"To see God's vision in your life and part of God's story. Right now, in your possession, you have a little extra resource, a talent, an asset, a gift ready to be given. You are blessed. You can be a blessing. There is a problem, an issue, hurt, a wound somewhere in the world that only you can heal no matter how inadequate you may feel. Your inner satisfaction, your ultimate fulfillment of your life purpose, and true happiness will never be fully unlocked until your unique gift and the world's unique needs come together. God's path for your life is a collision course; the intersection where your gift crashed into the world's need is where you will truly begin to live. Four simple promises: The Gift, The Need, The Journey, and the Joy are the keys that unlock God's story in your life. They will transform an ordinary life into an extraordinary adventure. Those four promises are indeed the beginning, but to tell the whole story, your journey to give your gift will break you, but it will also make you."

STACIE CALVIN

Aknowledgements

All Glory to The Creator. The security of Your guidance will allow me to carry my load with energy and confidence; I clothe myself with compassion, kindness, humility, gentleness and patience. Overall, these virtues I put on *love*, which binds them all together in perfect unity. I let the peace of Christ rule in my heart. I am thankful for Your grace and power of the Holy Spirit. Father, may Your will be done on earth in my life as it is in Heaven.

Thank You

Daryl and Denise O'Neil, Apostle over the tribe we call Ruach for challenging us that, "we all have a book in us" for your teachings, your service-driven hearts. We are representing Christ correctly in the earth.

Gateway Ministry Joy Lavender

Vicki Smith-Lockhart LPC Intern, MEd

Dr. Williams Lazarus House Initiative, Inc

Pam and Dan Booth

STACIE CALVIN

Kiesha King, Authoress Sylvia, LadyDes Dr. Makeba, Joyce SheRocksIt

Vince (Khalilah) Ivana, Glennis, Janine For Confirmation and Courage to let my story go.

Mama Margert Dorsey
Minister Willie Mooney (Ann)

My Four Pillars in Business
Melissa Boston, Phyllis Nash, Dr. Rita McGuire, Senator Patricia Van Belt #BlackGirlMagic

My Team Divine Diamonds

My Four Pillars in Life
My Two Most Life-Changing Challenging Gifts and MyFly, MyPinky #MyLegacy

My Family and Friends, the love and support given while on this journey with me; unspoken prayers. Much Love and Gratitude. You know who you are.

SHE Publishing Shenitha Burton, your support, knowledge and love poured out into A Sound Mind - Rebirth Project is the beginning of many. SHE publishing collaboration SASSY in the works! "Books holds the key to her career". Gratitude Queen, My SheroNitha, My Sister, Friend.

Non-profit Foundation for Still Birth and Premature Babies Mental Health.

A SOUND MIND

Meet the Author

Stacie P. Calvin, Author, Publisher, CEO of SASSY Publishing, A Mother, A GramMawMa, Certified Holistic Health Coach, Certified CBD Dispensary Owner /Operator, [Stacie Calvin - S.H.E. Publishing, LLC (shepublishingllc.com)](), TLKDispensary.wakanna.com

Sassy adj. describes a flirty, self-confident, loveable woman, yet elegant, classy and chic. Stacie has a real zest for life! Always finding something new to be excited about and enjoying the simplest things in life. Stacie has a huge heart, full of passion and kindness. An instinctive leader who guides with a whole heart and a beaming smile. She's overcome enough challenges to give first-rate suggestions and has enough energy to cheer up any friend. She applies her suggestions to her life. She is always encouraging you. Don't shrink your dreams. Elevate your courage and abilities.

www.ingramcontent.com/pod-product-compliance
Lightning Source LLC
Chambersburg PA
CBHW041215070526
44579CB00001B/2